To/

Take a trip back in time to the year you were born, 1961.

Happy 60th Birthday – enjoy reminiscing.

Lots of love,

WORLD MAP

World Population

3.07
BILLION

Britain population

52.6
MILLION

2021

World Population

7.8 BILLION

Britain population

67.61
MILLION

MAJOR WORLD LEADERS

UK- Prime Minister - Harold Macmillan, Prime Minister of the United Kingdom (1957–1963)

US PRESIDENT - Dwight D. Eisenhower, President of the United States (1953–1961)

John F. Kennedy, President of the United States (1961–1963)

RUSSIA/SOVIET UNION - Communist Party Leader - Nikita Khrushchev, First Secretary of the Communist Party of the Soviet Union (1953–1964)

SOUTH AFRICA - Prime Minister -- Hendrik Frensch Verwoerd

ITALY - Prime Minister - Amintore Fanfani, President of the Council of Ministers of Italy (1960–1963)

GERMANY - Chancellor -- Konrad Adenauer

FRANCE -- President -- Charles de Gaulle

CANADA - Prime Minister - John Diefenbaker, (1957–1963)

FRANCE - President - Charles de Gaulle, President of France (1959–1969)

You Have Been Loved for

60 years

Thats 720 months

3129 weeks | 21900 days

525600 hrs

31536000 minutes

1892160000 seconds
and counting...

60 & Fabulous

Alison Moyet	Martin Clunes
Barry McGuigan	Martin Kemp
Boy George	Mary King
Carol Smillie	Meera Syal
Daniel O'Donnell	Nicholas Lyndhurst
David Linley	Nicky Campbell
Diana Spencer	Ricky Gervais
Fiona Phillips	Robert Carlyle
Frank Bruno	Rory Bremner
Ian Rush	Steve McLaren
Jill Dando	Suggs
Joe Pasquale	Susan Boyle
Kerry Dixon	Tim Roth
Kevin Maguire	Wayne Hemingway
Marco Pierre White	William Hague

Oscars

ACTOR
WINNER

BURT LANCASTER
Elmer Gantry

ACTRESS
WINNER

ELIZABETH TAYLOR
Butterfield 8

CINEMATOGRAPHY
(COLOUR)
WINNER

SPARTACUS
Russell Metty

BEST MOTION
PICTURE WINNER

THE APARTMENT
Billy Wilder, Producer

SPECIAL EFFECTS
WINNER

THE TIME MACHINE
Visual Effects by Gene Warren,
Tim Baar

Films

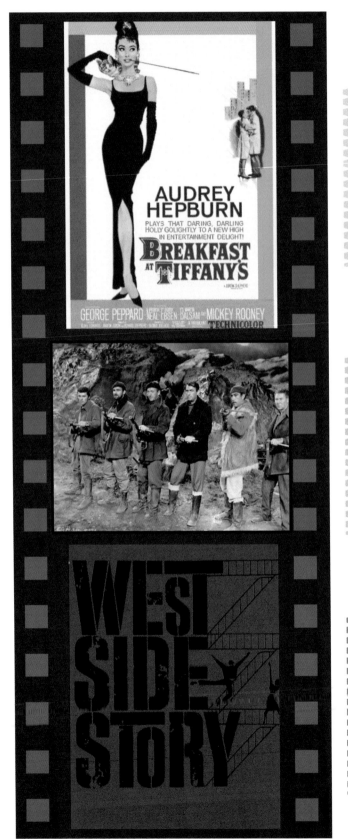

The infamous party scene took six days to film. The scene is pretty close to a real party - the extras were the Directors friends and they were supplied with real champagne, 120 gallons of soft drinks, 60 cartons of cigarettes, hot dogs, cold cuts, chips, dips, and sandwiches were involved. A smoker used by a beekeeper was brought in to create enough smoke.

The Guns of Navarone

Some members of the Greek royal family and their entourage were extras in the café scene, as they were visiting the set on the day that scene was being filmed. William Holden was the first actor sought to play Mallory. He asked for $750,000, plus 10% of the gross. He was turned down.

West Side Story

The most successful Oscar-winning musical of all time, beating the record Gigi (1958) set three years before. West Side Story won 10 Oscar awards (beating the 9 that Gigi won in '58).

Films 1961

- West Side Story starring Natalie wood, Richard Beymur, Rita Moreno & George Chakiris

- Breakfast at Tiffany's starring Audrey Hepburn & George Pappard

- Yojimbo starring Toshiro Mifuni, Tatsuya Nakadai

- Two Rode Together starring James Stewart , Richard Widmark & Linda Cristal

- A Taste of Honey starring dora Bryan & Rita Tushingham & Murray Melvin

- The Misfits starring clark gable & Marilyn Monroe

- West Side Story starring Natalie wood, Richard Beymur, Rita Moreno & russ Tamblyn

- The Guns of Navarone   Columbia Pictures

- The Parent Trap   Walt Disney/Buena Vista Distribution.

- The Absent-Minded Professor Walt Disney

- Lover Come Back   Universal Pictures.

- King of Kings   Metro-Goldwyn-Mayer

- One Hundred and One Dalmatians   Walt Disney/Buena Vista Distribution

- La Dolce Vita Cineriz/Pathé Consortium Cinéma

- Come September Universal pictures

Average cost of living 1961

Average House £2,403

in todays money thats £53,892

Average Salary £562

in todays money thats £12,604

Average Car price £805

in todays money thats £18,053

Average food shop £0.90

in todays money thats £20.92

Flour 1.5KG £0.10	£2.32 in todays money
Loaf of Bread £0.05	£1.16 in todays money
1KG Sugar £0.07	£1.63 in todays money
2.5KG Potatoes £0.08	£1.86 in todays money
1pt Milk £0.13	£3.02 in todays money
400g Bacon £0.26	£6.04 in todays money
250g Butter £0.08	£1.86 in todays money
400g Cheese £0.12	£2.79 in todays money

The Terra Nova Islands were discovered in 1961 by an Australian research expedition, but when geologists went to map them in 1989, they found no islands because they don't exist.

The Antarctic Treaty of 1961 which recognises no sovereign claim of Antarctica, prohibits mining, military activity & only allows scientific activity on the continent. Article V specifically prohibits any nuclear explosions in Antarctica and the disposal of any radioactive waste material there.

Coca-Cola ads from the forties gave Santa Claus a sidekick named Sprite Boy named because he was a Sprite. The drink was named after the character which was introduced in 1961.

Mastering The Art Of French Cooking is published in September 1961. The cookbook is an instant success and made Julia Childs a star for years to come.

Barbie gets her first boyfriend. Ken is introduced in March.

Music

Every decade has memorable music and a distinct sound that defines the age and becomes part of the fabric of peoples lives through shared memories. The 1960s perhaps more than any other. It would be impossible to succinctly cover the music scene that adequately reflected the impact of the music on those that grew up in the 60s. While rock music began in the 50s it was in the 60s that it really came into its own. Even youngsters today will likely know the biggest bands of the 60s which include: The Beatles, The Rolling Stones, The Velvet Underground, The Who, The Doors, Frank Zappa, Jimi Hendrix, Led Zeppelin, The Kinks, Pink Floyd, The Beach Boys, The Kinks and many many more. The impact of these huge bands can easily be seen in the success of the artists throughout every decade since.

Born in 61' you'll be lucky enough to remember the excitement of going to a record shop and finding that perfect song you've been desperate to listen to. Crowded in your room with your friends, the first few notes from your vinyl player flooding the room with emotion like you've never felt. While the benefits of technology are plentiful, for example thousands of tracks available instantly on download It's hard to imagine the same effect from a music streaming service.

What was the number 1 on the day you were born? Look at the table below to find out.

1st January - Johnny Tilliston, Poetry in Motion - held for 3 weeks.

22nd January - Elvis Presley, Are You Lonesome Tonight - held 4 weeks.

19th February - Everly Brothers, Walk Right Back - held 4 weeks.

19th March - Elvis Presley, Wooden Heart - held for 3 weeks.

9th April - The Allisons, Are You Sure? Held for 2 weeks.

23rd April Elvis Presley Wooden Heart - held for 1 week.

30th April - The Temperance Seven, You're Driving Me Crazy - held for 1 week.

7th May - Marcels, Blue Moon - held for 2 weeks.

21st May - Del Shannon, Runaway - held for 1 week.

28th May - Elvis Presley, Surrender - held for 4 weeks.

25th June - Del Shannon, Runaway - held for 1 week.

2nd July - Everly Brothers, Temptation - held for 4 weeks.

30th July - Eden Kane, Well I Ask You - held for 1 week.

6th August - Helen Shapiro, You Don't Know - held for 2 weeks.

20th August - John Leyton, Johnny Remember Me - held for 5 weeks.

24th September - The Shadows, Kon-Tiki - held for 1 week.

1st October - The Highwaymen, Michael Row the Boat - held for 1 week.

8th October - Helen Shapiro, Walkin' Back to Happiness - held for 4 weeks.

5th November - Elvis Presley, His Latest Flame - held for 3 weeks.

26th November - Bobby Vee, Take Good Care of my Baby - held for 1 week.

3rd December - Frankie Vaughan, Tower of Strength - held for 4 weeks.

31st December - Acker Bilk, Stranger on the Shore - held for 2 weeks.

The Beatles began with Lennon and McCartney, who first performed together in Liverpool in 1957. 3 years later The Beatles were founded in Liverpool in 1960. The four piece (comprising John Lennon, Paul McCartney, George Harrison and Ringo Starr) broke up in 1970. It was a decade of music that would impact the music industry forever.

The first Beatles song to chart in the UK was Love Me Do in 1962, their first No1 hit single came a year later 'From Me To You. The Beatles had 17 No1 hits, 28 UK top tens, 38 UK top 40s, with 65 weeks at No 1, 188 weeks in top 10 and 365 weeks in the top 40.

Beatlemania described the fanaticism that the band created, and the international success in America was unlike anything any other British band had experienced. This was named the 'British Invasion' as the Beatles led the way for an influx of British music in America.

The Who formed in 1964 in London. Formed of Pete Townshend, bass guitarist and singer John Entwistle, and drummer Keith Moon. They have sold over 100 million records worldwide. Despite this success they have never had a UK no 1 single (though they have held No 1 spot for an album) In the UK they have had 14 top 10s, 25 top 40s with 43 weeks in the top 10s, and 194 weeks in the top 40s.

Pink Floyd

Pink Floyd formed in Gaining an early the first British Pink Floyd were students Syd Barrett Nick Mason (drums), guitar, vocals), and (keyboards, vocals). London in 1965. following as one of psychedelic groups, founded by (guitar, lead vocals), Roger Waters (bass Richard Wright

Pink Floyd are one of the rock bands of all time. The The Wall are among the best- both have been inducted into the greatest progressive Dark Side of the Moon and selling albums of all time, and Grammy Hall of Fame. However, despite all their success to date In the UK they have had just 1 single to hit the UK No 1 spot, however they did have 6 No 1 albums. The group have sold over 250 million albums worldwide.

The Rolling Stones

Formed in 1962, the Stones offered a grittier sound to the pop rock of the 60s. Today they have an estimated 240 million record sales, this makes them one of the best selling artists of all time. This accolade ensured their space in the Rock and Roll Hall of Fame in 1989 and later in the UK Hall of Fame 2004. In total they have released a whopping 30 albums! They have also been awarded 3 Grammy awards and a Grammy lifetime achievement award.

Fashion

Fashion of the 60's became much more relaxed and casual. This trend was seen across all age groups and genders.

There are broad themes that encapsulate the trends of the 60s; 'Jackie O' style and the ladylike elegance continued from the 50's, new boundary challenging styles from designers like Mary Quant along with space age influences, and of course the "hippie style".

Changes in Menswear saw a move away from the standard uniform and limited choices of the 50's. Pattern, texture, colour all things normally reserved from womenswear were suddenly acceptable in mens fashion designs. The changing boundaries of fashion reflected the changes in society.

Media attention on small groups of young people within cities helped popularise the new trends and they swept throughout Britain. Examples of these new styles were mini-skirts, culottes, go-go boots, PVC clothes and other experimental styles.

The distinctive 'look' of the 60s is epitomised in Mary Quant mini skirts, Jackie Kennedy pill box hat, huge doe eyes with false eyelashes promoted by models such as Twiggy. Hairstyles also followed the experimental line and new styles and lengths followed the fashion styles of the day.

The 'hippie movement' saw psychedelic prints, bright neon colours and mismatched patters with floral motifs.

In the early to mid 60's 'Modernists' known as 'Mods' was the biggest influence of young male fashion. Music and fashion intertwined reflected the desires of each sub-culture.

Fashion

100% European Hair

A	B	C
Band Wig $29.99 Up or $3 a month	"Scamp" Cut $64.99 or $5 a month	Crowning Glory $34.99 Up or $3 a month

Our Best Wigs...With Real Human Hair

WIGS in natural hair colors and fashion shades

Actual Colors may vary slightly from printed colors

D
Versatile Switch
$3.99

SYNTHETIC FIBERS IN [D], [E], F and [G]
LOOK, FEEL, ACT LIKE HUMAN HAIR

F
THE "GAMIN"
$4.99
Also in Girls' Sizes
$3.99

Pre Styled Wigs

G
THE "CLEOPATRA"
$8.99
Also in Girls' Sizes
$4.99

BUDGET BEATING BEAUTIES

1482 & 1483 . . . AS-CAN-BE . . . casual elegance of this V-neck, rayon linen sheath, cut to pencil-slim proportions . . . and you'll love the tiny price! Smart elasticized waist gaily banded with a marshmallow white belt aglitter with gold color keys. Back kick pleat. Washable. Pink, Lime, Turquoise (all shown) or Black.
1482 . . . Misses sizes 8, 10, 12, 14, 16, 18.   **499**
1483 . . . Half sizes 14½, 16½, 18½, 20½, 22½.   **599**

1484 . . . FLOWERS 'A BLOOM . . . gaily sprouting in flower pots all around the border and bodice of this delightful striped cotton percale pretty. The full skirt boasts big, handy pockets that are perked with piping, as is the round neckline. Red (shown) or Blue print.
Misses sizes 12, 14, 16, 18, 20.
Half sizes 14½, 16½, 18½, 20½, 22½, 24½.   **399**

1485 . . . YOU'LL WANT A DOZEN . . . summer coolers like this striped pretty of drip-dry, wrinkle-shy acetate jersey! Perky bow accents scoop neck bodice that buttons to the waist and flows into a softly pleated skirt. Orange/White (shown), Blue/White or Green/White stripe.
Misses sizes 12, 14, 16, 18, 20.
Half sizes 14½, 16½, 18½, 20½, 22½.   **599**

1486 . . . A-BLOOM WITH FASHION . . . a thrilling dress of silky cotton and rayon Cuprioni. Garlands of flowers sparkle on a scoop neck lovely that's set afloat with whirls of unpressed pleats. Chic leather-look novelty belt ties with a bouncy bow. Back zipper. Rose (shown), Mint Green or Blue, all with White.
Misses sizes 12, 14, 16, 18, 20.
Half sizes 16½, 18½, 20½, 22½, 24½.   **699**

1487 . . . CHECKED FOR SMARTNESS . . . and iced with a white yoke that's sweetened with Schiffli embroidery. Of washable cotton gingham that drips-dry. Snapped trim an

70

Sports

BOXING

- June 3rd in Los Angeles - Emile Griffith knocked out Gaspar Ortega to retain championship.

CYCLING

- August 1 - death of Adrie Voorting (aged 30), Dutch cyclist.

- Giro d'Italia won by Ercole Baldini of Italy Tour de France - Jacques Anquetil of France

- UCI Road World Championships - Men's road race - Rik Van Looy of Belgium

FIGURE SKATING

- The World Figure Skating Championships in Prague are cancelled after the entire USA team are killed in an aircrash.

GOLF

Men's professional

- Masters Tournament - Gary Player becomes the first international golfer to win the Masters.

- U.S. Open - Gene Littler

- The Open - Arnold Palmer

- PGA Championship - Jerry Barber

- PGA Tour money leader - Gary Player -

- Ryder Cup - United States wins 14½ to 9½ over Britain in team golf.

Women's professional

Women's Western Open - Mary Lena Faulk

- LPGA Championship - Mickey Wright

- U.S. Women's Open - Mickey Wright

- Titleholders Championship - Mickey Wright

- LPGA Tour money leader - Mickey Wright -

Men's amateur

British Amateur - Michael Bonallack

U.S. Amateur - Jack Nicklaus

HORSE RACING

Steeplechases

- Cheltenham Gold Cup - Saffron Tartan

- Grand National - Nicolaus Silver

Flat races

- Australia - Melbourne Cup won by Lord Fury

- Canada - Queen's Plate won by Blue Light

- France - Prix de l'Arc de Triomphe won by Molvedo

- Ireland - Irish Derby Stakes won by Your Highness

English Triple Crown Races:

1	2,000 Guineas Stakes - Rockavon
2	The Derby - Psidium
3	St. Leger Stakes - Aurelius

United States Triple Crown Races:

1	Kentucky Derby - Carry Back
2	Preakness Stakes - Carry Back
3	Belmont Stakes - Sherluck

1961

FOOTBALL

Britain

- FA Cup final – Tottenham Hotspur 2-0 Leicester City.

RUGBY UNION

- 67th Five Nations Championship series is won by France

RUGBY LEAGUE

- 1960–61 Northern Rugby Football League season

Leeds won their first Championship when they defeated Warrington 25-10 in the play-off final.

The Challenge Cup winners were St. Helens who beat Wigan 12-6.

TENNIS

England

- Wimbledon Men's Singles Championship – Rod Laver (Australia) defeats Chuck McKinley (USA) 6–3, 6–1, 6–4

- Wimbledon Women's Singles Championship – Angela Mortimer Barrett (Great Britain) defeats Christine Truman Janes (Great Britain) 4–6, 6–4, 7–5

TV news 1961

7th January, The Avengers premieres on ITV.

3rd February, The final live episode of Coronation Street is aired. From now on all episodes are
prerecorded. The next live transmission is the 8th December 2000.

6th March, Scheduling change for Coronation Street begins airing on Monday and Wednesday evenings at 7.30pm. Previously, it had been transmitted on Wednesday and Friday evenings at 7pm.

March An edition of ABC's Sunday evening religious programme The Sunday Break causes controversy by showing Jesus wearing a pair of jeans.

4th April, Southern launches a weeknight 30 minute regional news programme called Day By Day.

29th April, Westward Television, the first ITV franchise for South West England, goes on air.

1st September, Border Television, the ITV franchise for the English-Scottish Border and Isle of Man,
goes on air.

30th September, Grampian Television, the ITV franchise for North East Scotland, goes on air.

1st October, Songs of Praise, featuring Christian congregations singing hymns, debuts on BBC Television.

2nd October, Points of View Debut

15th December, The BBC broadcasts the first Comedy Playhouse.

Christmas Eve 1961		BBC Christmas day 1961		Boxing Day 1961	
10.00am	Ar Gyger Heddiw'r Bore	9.30am	Good Christian Men, Rejoice	11.22am	The Red Balloon
	a programme of carols	10.00am	Sambo and the Snow Mountains	11.55am	Juke Box Jury
10.30am	Morning Service	10.30am	O Come, All Ye Faithful		a new disc-a Hit or a Miss?
11.30am	Elsa, the Lioness	11.30am	Max Bygraves	12.30pm	Boxing Day Grandstand
12.00	On the Twelfth Day	12.20pm	Citizen James		including Motor Racing
12.20pm	Seeing and Believing	12.50pm	Be My Guest	5.00pm	The Princess and the Pea
12.40pm	Mountain Pastures	1.25pm	Tenderfoot	5.50pm	The News
1.00pm	Welcome Christmas	2.10pm	Appeal	5.55pm	Today's Sport
1.30pm	No Room for Wild Animals	2.15pm	The Christmas Music	6.00pm	Town and Around
2.30pm	The Singing Years	3.00pm	The Queen Her Majesty's recorded Christmas Message to the Commonwealth	6.05pm	Here's Harry
3.00pm	Brian Rix presents...			6.30pm	Cinderella
	"Flat Spin, a farce"	3.07pm	Billy Smart's Circus		from the Wimbledon Theatre, London starring Dickie Valentine and Jill Day
4.25pm	Quillow and the Giant	4.05pm	The World of Walt Disney		
5.20pm	Overland Trail	5.15pm	Film : Just William's Luck (1947	8.00pm	Brian Rix presents...
6.10pm	The News	6.45pm	The News		"Will Any Gentlemen?"
6.15pm	A Festival of Carols	6.55pm	Christmas at Canterbury	9.30pm	The News
7.05pm	What Manner of Child...	7.25pm	This Is Your Life	9.40pm	Maigret
7.25pm	What's My Line?	8.00pm	The Black and White Minstrel Show		A Crime for Christmas
	Chairman, Eamonn Andrews	9.00pm	Film: Rebecca (1940)	10.30pm	Film: I'll Be Seeing You
7.55pm	Billy Cotton Band Show	11.05pm	Late Night News		starring Ginger Rogers Joseph Gotten with Shirley Temple
8.40pm	Sunday Night Play	11.10pm	Television Dancing Club	11.55pm	The Weather Man
10.25pm	The News		special Christmas edition		Closedown
10.30pm	Peter Ustinov	11.55pm	The Power of Gentleness		
11.30pm	Tibor Varga	12.00	The Weather Man		
11.55pm	Midnight Mass of the Nativity		Closedown		
1.30am	Closedown	10.55am	Telewele		
9.29am	Headline News	11.20am	Headline News		

Popular 60s TV Shows

Doctor Who is a British science fiction television programme produced by the BBC since 1963. The world's longest running science fiction programme, Doctor Who first aired in 1963 and continued until 1989.

DAD'S ARMY a BBC sitcom about the British militia called the Home Guard. Broadcast from 1968 to 1977, it ran for nine series and had 80 episodes in total.

CORONATION STREET One of Britain's most successful soap operas first premiered in 1960 and is still running today.

Thunderbirds Thunderbirds are go! Gerry and Sylvia Anderson's marionette animated series ran between 1965 to 1966

The British Invasion wasn't confined to music. The spy craze led to British television productions being shown on American networks. Here were shows produced in the U.K. and shown in America on networks on primetime:

The Avengers an espionage television programme, created in 1961, that ran for 161 episodes until 1969

The Baron series made in 1965 and 1966, based on the book series by John Creasey

The Champions espionage thriller/science fiction/occult detective fiction adventure And consists of 30 episodes broadcast on the UK network ITV during 1968 to 1969.

Journey to the Unknown aired on ABC in 1968 to 1969 and then aired in the UK on ITV during 1969.

Man in a Suitcase private eye thriller series produced by Lew Grade's ITC Entertainment. It originally aired in the United Kingdom on ITV from 27 September 1967 to 17 April 1968.

The Prisoner a 1967 British avant-garde social science fiction television series about an unnamed British intelligence agent who is abducted and imprisoned in a mysterious coastal village

The Saint a British ITC mystery spy thriller that aired in the UK between 1962 and 1969.

Secret Agent aired in Uk between 1960 and 1962,

10 Most Popular Baby Names - 1961

Michael	Mary
David	Lisa
John	Susan
James	Linda
Robert	Karen
Mark	Patricia
William	Donna
Richard	Cynthia
Thomas	Sandra
Steven	Deborah

Books published 1961

Catch-22

by Joseph Heller

James and the Giant Peach

by Roald Dahl

Where the Red Fern Grows

by Wilson Rawls

Stranger in a Strange Land

by Robert A. Heinlein

The Phantom Tollbooth

by Norton Juster

Mother Night

by Kurt Vonnegut Jr.

Revolutionary Road

by Richard Yates

Solaris

by Stanisław Lem

Go, Dog. Go!

by P.D. Eastman

Mastering the Art of French Cooking

by Julia Child

Black Like Me

by John Howard Griffin

Memories, Dreams, Reflections

by C.G. Jung

The Sneetches and Other Stories

by Dr. Seuss

The Winter of Our Discontent

by John Steinbeck

The Prime of Miss Jean Brodie

by Muriel Spark

The Wretched of the Earth

by Frantz Fanon

The Complete Tales and Poems of Winnie-the-Pooh 1-4

by A.A. Milne

The Snows of Kilimanjaro

by Ernest Hemingway

60s Toys

1961: Barbie finally has a boyfriend, Ken, measured exactly half inch taller than Barbie. Makers Mattel faced dilemma, should Ken be anatomically correct below the waist? Some unremovable 'perma-pants' solved their problem. Scalextric, took off and enjoyed a boom year in 1961 when it was the third best selling toy, just behind Noddy.

1962: saw the arrival of Mousetrap with its catchphrase 'It's fun to build this comical wonder, but woe to the mouse who gets caught under'. Kit modelling became really popular and Airfix was one of 1962's top toys

1963: saw this girl next door look the Sindy doll arrived, marketed as 'the doll you love to dress' she just flew off the shelves for Christmas. Diplomacy, a board game, that required cunning and skill proved to be a top selling game and Matchbox

1964: This is the year MR Potato lost his real potato body and gained a new plastic one. Toy doll so the Beatles were also a huge hit amidst the Beatlemania.

1965: A new award this year - the James Bond Aston Martin Car. The craze for spy films made its way to the toy market with little boys everywhere aspiring to become 007.

1966: Britains first doll for boys is released this year, Action Man. You will most certainly have had one of this years most popular new toys, the Spirograph. Hours of fun doodling away.

1967: Some real toy classics from this year. Etch-a-sketch, Kerplunk and wargame Battleships was the top of Christmas lists.

1968: Sindy doll is more popular than Barbie and wins toy of the year. Fisher Price toy Snoopy can be seen in many a families Christmas photos as it was a hugely popular toy with toddlers who delighted pulling him along on his plastic lead. For slightly older boys, Batman utility belt was the accessory to have.

1969: Hot Wheels cars feature numerous times on the top spot of kids favourite toys from the 1960s all the way to present day. The only change might be that it is now on the top spot with girls and boys which may have been less likely back in the 60's.

Do you remember?

Popular 60s Children's TV shows

Biggles - a 1960s television series based on the Biggles series of books by W.E. Johns. Neville Whiting starred in the show.

Animal Magic - a BBC children's television series which ran from 1962 to 1983 from BBC. It began fortnightly moving to weekly in 1964.

Belle and Sebastian is a 1965 French TV children's serial based on the 1965 novel Belle et Sébastien by Cécile Aubry. It was 13 episodes long and starred Aubry's son Mehdi as Sebastien.

Bizzy Lizzy - a British children's TV series from the 1960s. Bizzy Lizzy was a little girl whose dress had a magic flower. When she touched it, her wishes came true – but if she made more than four wishes in a day, all her previous wishes were undone. Her first wish each day was to make her Eskimo doll, Little Mo, come to life.

Bleep and Booster - a children's cartoon series by William Timym (pronounced Tim) originally shown on the BBC's Blue Peter. A total of 313 five-minute episodes were released between 1964 and 1977.

Camberwick Green - a British children's television series that ran from January to March 1966 on BBC1, featuring stop motion puppets. Camberwick Green is the first in the Trumptonshire trilogy, which also includes Trumpton and Chigley.

Crackerjack - aired every year from 1955 to 1984 with the exception of 1971. You'll likely have strong memories of this popular kids variety show.

The Clangers is a stop-motion animation cartoon about a group of mouse like creatures who live on the moon. They converse in a whistle like voice and eat only green soup and blue string pudding (prepared by the Soup Dragon).

Trumpton 1967 BBC1

Pingwings 1961-64

Magpie 1968 ITV

Watch with Mother 1952-1975

Crackerjack 1955-1984

The Herbs 1968

Jackanory 1965-1996

Blue Peter 1958 - present day.
Longest running kids TV
programme in the world

Do you
remember?

World Events

1st May 1961

Betting had been restricted in the Uk since 1853. Underground betting was common with illegal shops set up all through the UK.

R.A.Butler announced a plan to legalise betting in 1960, advocating the benefit of strict controls. This proposal was supported by the Archbishop of Canterbury.

Unexpectedly, one of the key arguments in favour (which was the benefit of increased tax to the Government) was not actually introduced until 1966. Betting shops became legal in May 1961. Within the year more than 10,000 shops had set up in business.

1961 Apollo programme (25th May)

President Kennedy announces his vision and goal to put a man on the moon before the end of the decade.

Bay of Pigs

April 1961

The mission to invade Cuba through the Bay of Pigs fails. President Kennedy accepts responsibility. The invasion by Cuban exiles was backed by the US government as an attempt to overthrow Fidel Castro.

Strobogrammatic Year 1961

The first strobogrammatic year since 1881. So termed for a year where the numbers that form the year look the same upside down. You are unique in being born in a strobogrammatic year as there will not be another one for thousands of years to come (6009).

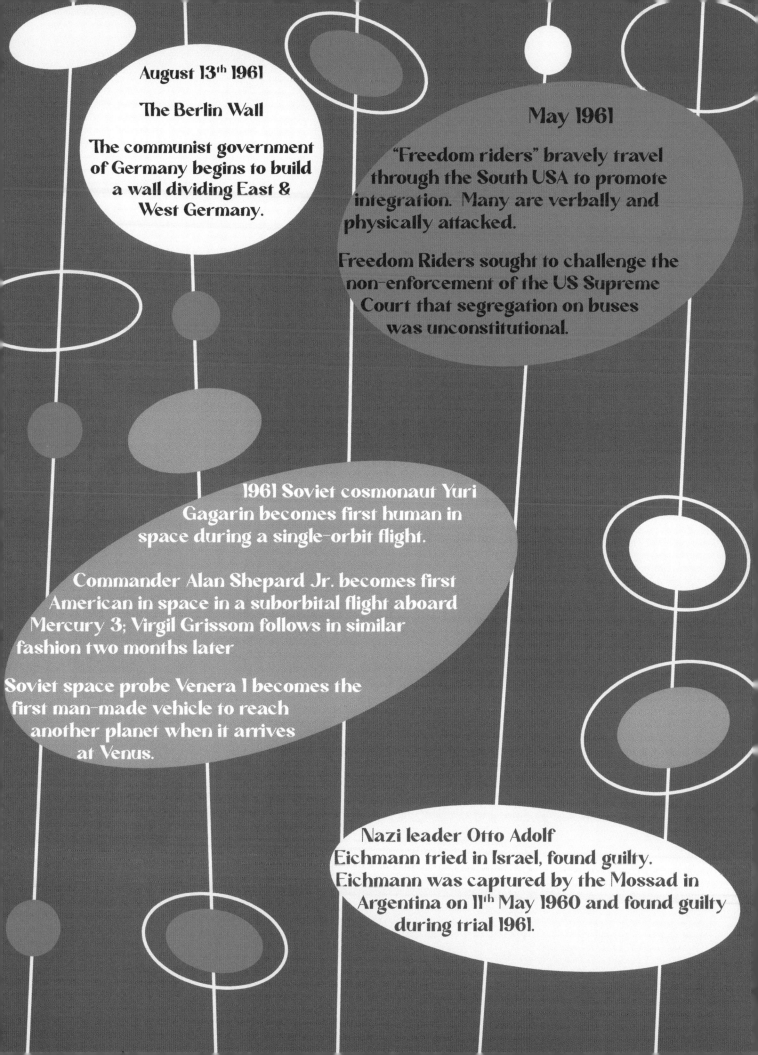

August 13th 1961

The Berlin Wall

The communist government of Germany begins to build a wall dividing East & West Germany.

May 1961

"Freedom riders" bravely travel through the South USA to promote integration. Many are verbally and physically attacked.

Freedom Riders sought to challenge the non-enforcement of the US Supreme Court that segregation on buses was unconstitutional.

1961 Soviet cosmonaut Yuri Gagarin becomes first human in space during a single-orbit flight.

Commander Alan Shepard Jr. becomes first American in space in a suborbital flight aboard Mercury 3; Virgil Grissom follows in similar fashion two months later

Soviet space probe Venera 1 becomes the first man-made vehicle to reach another planet when it arrives at Venus.

Nazi leader Otto Adolf Eichmann tried in Israel, found guilty. Eichmann was captured by the Mossad in Argentina on 11th May 1960 and found guilty during trial 1961.

1961 Events

January 9th British authorities announce they have uncovered a large soviet spy ring, the Portland Spy Ring.

January 20th John F. Kennedy is sworn in as the 35th President of the United States.

Jan 25th Disney's One Hundred and One Dalmatians is released in cinemas.

January 31st Ham the Chimp, a 37-pound (17-kg) male, is launched aboard Mercury-Redstone 2, in a test of the Project Mercury Spacecraft.

February 9th The Beatles perform for the first time at The Cavern Club.

February 12th The USSR launches Venera 1 towards Venus.

Feb 15th A total solar eclipse occurs in the southern part of Europe.

March 1st United States President John F. Kennedy establishes the Peace Corps.

March 13th Black and white 5 notes cease to be legal tender in the UK.

April 12th Vostok 1: Soviet cosmonaut Yuri Gagarin becomes the first human in space, orbiting the Earth once before parachuting to the ground.

May 5th Mercury program: Alan Shepard becomes the first American in space, aboard Mercury-Redstone 3.

May 15th J. Heinrich Matthaei alone performs the Poly-U-Experiment, and is the first person to recognise the genetic code..

June 23rd The Antarctic Treaty comes into effect.

1961 Events

September 7th Tom and Jerry make a return with their first episode since 1958, Switchin' Kitten. The new creator, Gene Deitch, makes 12 more Tom and Jerry episodes.

In the U.S, the Walt Disney anthology television series, renamed Walt Disney's Wonderful World of Color, moves from ABC to NBC.

October 10th A volcanic eruption on Tristan da Cunha results in the whole population to be evacuated to Britain 1963.

October 12th The death penalty is abolished in New Zealand.

October 17th Paris massacre of 1961: French police in Paris attack about 30,000 protesting a curfew applied only to Algerians.

October 25th The first edition of Private Eye, the British satirical magazine, is published.

October 30th -Nuclear weapons testing: The Soviet Union detonates a 58-megaton yield hydrogen bomb known as Tsar Bomba.

November 9th Robert White records a world air speed record of 4,093 mph

November 14th Yves Saint Laurent, a luxury fashion brand of France is founded.

December 2nd Cold War: In a nationally broadcast speech, Cuban leader Fidel Castro announces he is a Marxist Leninist.

Dec 11th - American involvement in the Vietnam War officially begins, as the first American helicopters arrive in Saigon,

December 14th Walt Disney's first live-action Technicolor musical, Babes in Toyland is released, it is not a hit.

December 31st Ireland's first national television station, Telefís Éireann (later RTÉ) broadcasts.

60s Inventions

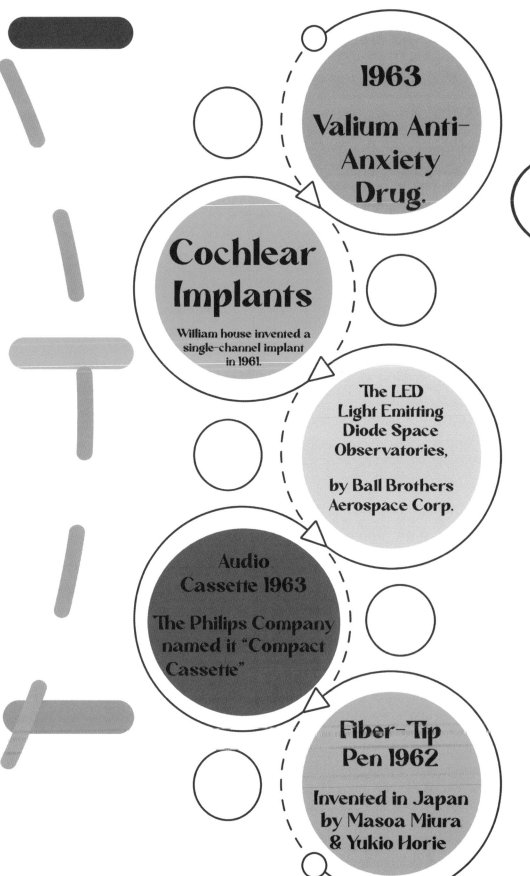

1963

Valium Anti-Anxiety Drug.

Cochlear Implants

William house invented a single-channel implant in 1961.

The LED Light Emitting Diode Space Observatories,

by Ball Brothers Aerospace Corp.

Audio Cassette 1963

The Philips Company named it "Compact Cassette"

Fiber-Tip Pen 1962

Invented in Japan by Masoa Miura & Yukio Horie

Lava Lamp

In 1963, Edward Green invented the lava lamp. At the time he called it the 'Astro Lamp". The exact formula is a secret however this has since been replicated by many companies as the popularity of lava lamps remain strong. Heat from the wax melts the wax that floats up and down in the water-based liquid. The ingredient tetrachloride keeps the buoyant wax heavy enough to keep sinking.

Spacewar
the first
Computer Video
Game- 1962

Cashpoint
First used in the UK 1967

1961
Silicone
Breast
Implants

Bubble Wrap

A great example of an accidental invention. The inventors, Alfred Fielding and Marc Chavannes were trying to create a textured wallpaper. They were initially discouraged by the air that kept trapping between the plastic layers. In 1960, they founded the sealed Air Corporation but were still trying to find a good use for this material they had produced. Little known to them that technology of another kind would give them their solution. IBM released the 1401 computer and needed a safe way to ship the fragile computer. They realised immediately what the purpose of their plastic air wrap should be and the rest they say, is history.

60s Inventions

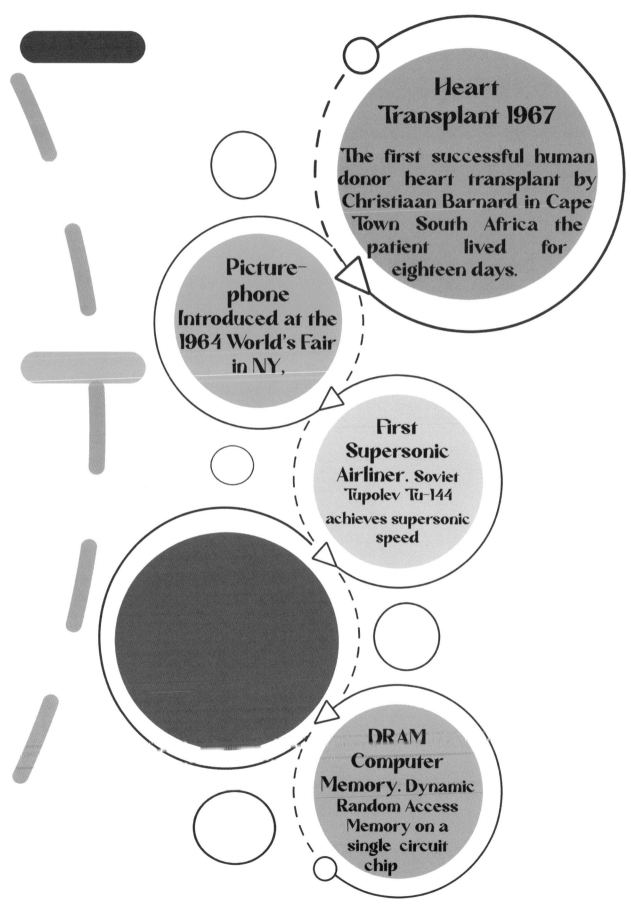

Heart Transplant 1967

The first successful human donor heart transplant by Christiaan Barnard in Cape Town South Africa the patient lived for eighteen days.

Picture-phone Introduced at the 1964 World's Fair in NY,

First **Supersonic Airliner.** Soviet Tupolev Tu-144 achieves supersonic speed

DRAM Computer Memory. Dynamic Random Access Memory on a single circuit chip

Aspartame

Stories of inventions are often surprising. Aspartame is one of those that came into existence when chemist James M.Schlatter licked his finger to turn a piece of paper. He had been working on anti-ulcer drugs and had managed to get some of the synthesised product on his hand. Finding out it had an incredibly sweet taste he knew this could have other uses. It wasn't approved until 1981.

Kevlar

Continuing our theme of amazing accidental discoveries, Poly-paraphenylene terephthalamide (Kevlar). In 1964, the company was trying to find a way to make strong but lightweight tyres. Stephanie Kwolek created a mixture that did not have the attributes they were looking for. Stephanie decided to dry the mixture and found it was extremely strong. This amazing invention has saved the lives of many people since the 1960s and continues to be sued today.

Countertop microwave oven.

Introduced in 1967 by the Amana corporation.

Swinging Sixties

The decade you grew up in was a youth-driven cultural revolution. Britain was changing, the change started by those who had grown up in the 40s and 50s. We can see the impact of a generation free from conscription but who remember the war and the scarcity that accompanied the conflict.

As technology developed the economy improved and we see families being able to enjoy leisure activities. The typical sixties recalled as the 'Swinging sixties' would have been reflective of urban cities with concentrated groups of young people involved in music, arts and fashion. For many people this doesn't align with their memories of everyday life however it was still hugely influential.

While the fifties saw the birth of the teenager it is really in the 60s that we see young people with a voice. The social and economic climate allows a creativity of expression that wasn't possible previously. Parents looking to see their children enjoy themselves saw teenagers that were significantly different to any other generation.

Arguably more than any other decade in the 20th Century the 60s was most revolutionary. The increased levels in employment saw an economic boom. This in turn affects the appetite for new technology. Television and pocket transistor radios allowed people to spend their time listening to music or watching shows on television. The colour TV license was introduced in 1968 and cost £10 (although colour TV sets didn't outnumber black & white until 1978 due to the high cost). By 1969 it is estimated that just 200,000 households owned a colour tv - if you did you were one of the lucky few!

Overall looking at the decade of the 60s there is an air of optimism, a 'we can do anything' aspiration with the race to the Moon, thriving music scene, the British Invasion and British fashion subcultures paving the way for modern design. By the end of the decade, Neil Armstrong & Buzz Aldrin achieved the impossible by becoming the first men to land on the moon (1969). In start contrast to the battered and bruised Britain of the 50s the 60s had a sense that anything was possible.

Pop Art

The pop art movement has it roots in the 1950s and went on to become synonymous with the 1960s. It originally began in Britain and American and then inspired artists from all over the world to contribute. It reflected the changes in society particularly from young people who were challenging the many traditions and expectations in their lives. In 1957 pop artist Richard Hamilton listed the characteristics of pop art in a letter to his friends:

"Pop Art is: Popular (designed for a mass audience) Transient (short-term solution), Expendable (easily forgotten), low cost (mass produced, young, witty, sexy, Gimmicky, Glamorous, Big business"

Andy Warhol

The canned soup image is one of the most well known pop art prints. Andy Warhol used images from everyday media and consumer products to make his art pieces. He first exhibited the Campbells soup in 1962.

We hope you enjoyed your gift. We have another waiting for you...

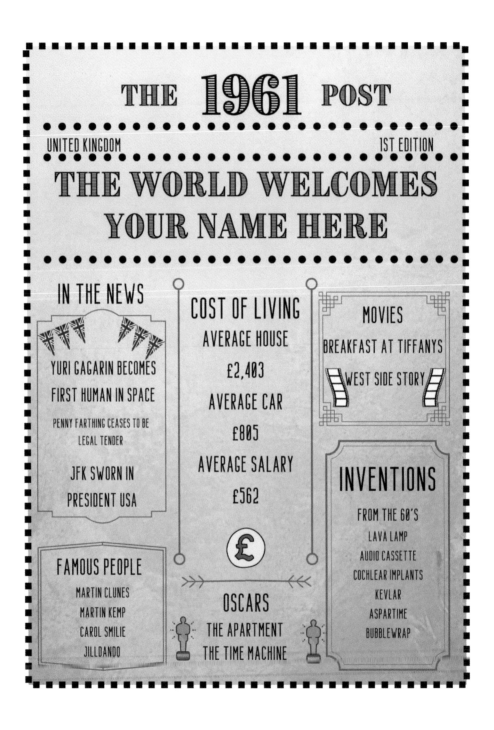

THE **1961** POST

UNITED KINGDOM   1ST EDITION

THE WORLD WELCOMES YOUR NAME HERE

IN THE NEWS

YURI GAGARIN BECOMES FIRST HUMAN IN SPACE

PENNY FARTHING CEASES TO BE LEGAL TENDER

JFK SWORN IN PRESIDENT USA

COST OF LIVING

AVERAGE HOUSE
£2,403

AVERAGE CAR
£805

AVERAGE SALARY
£562

MOVIES

BREAKFAST AT TIFFANYS

WEST SIDE STORY

INVENTIONS

FROM THE 60'S
LAVA LAMP
AUDIO CASSETTE
COCHLEAR IMPLANTS
KEVLAR
ASPARTIME
BUBBLEWRAP

FAMOUS PEOPLE

MARTIN CLUNES
MARTIN KEMP
CAROL SMILIE
JILL DANDO

OSCARS

THE APARTMENT
THE TIME MACHINE

Little Pips Press

How to claim your free gift:

Visit the following address:

https://www.subscribepage.com/littlepipspress

Type in your email to receive your link to download the editable poster that you can print out at home or at a local printers. Whether your celebrating at home or elsewhere this will help make an occasion of your special day. This can also be framed as a memento of your special day.

The poster can be edited to include your name and can be printed any size.

Little Pips Press is a family run business. Our range of milestone books includes:

We hope you have a great Birthday!

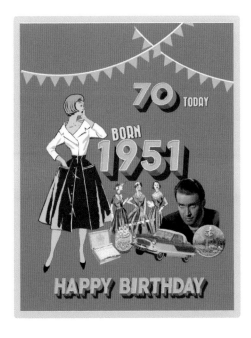

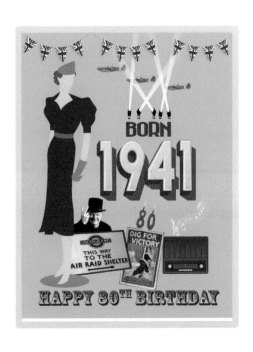

The legal stuff

Attribution for photo images goes to the following talented photographers under the creative commons licenses specified:

Printed in Great Britain
by Amazon